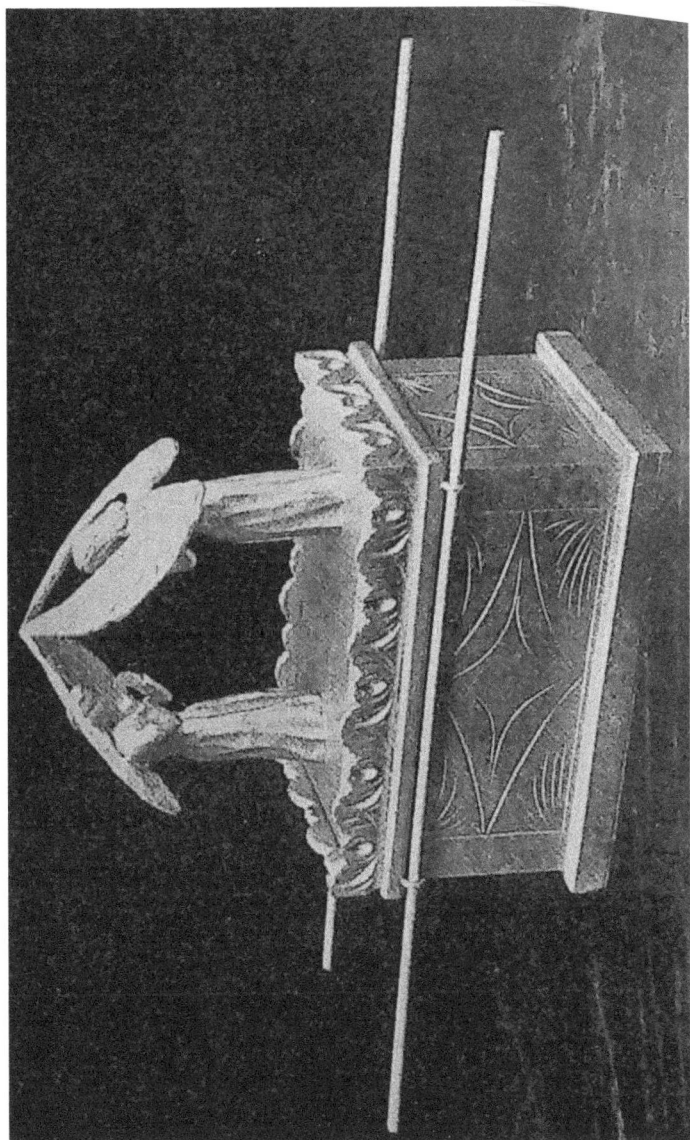

THE ARK OF THE COVENANT

THE
MYSTERY
OF THE FATE OF THE
ARK OF THE COVENANT

CYRIL C. DOBSON

ISBN 978-2-925369-04-2
Printed in the USA.

www.ultimatumeditions.com

ULTIMATUM
E   D   I   T   I   O   N   S

My warm thanks are due to Sir Charles Marston for information, sympathy, and guidance in the research that has been entailed in compiling this work.

Cyril C. Dobson

CONTENTS

_____

CHAPTERS

APPENDICES

ILLUSTRATIONS

CHAPTER I

INTRODUCTORY: THE ARK NOT CARRIED TO BABYLON, NOR DESTROYED IN THE BURNING OF THE TEMPLE

In 584 B.C. Jerusalem, including the Temple, was burnt to the ground by the forces of Nebuchadnezzar, under the command of Nebuzaradan. As no mention is made in Biblical records as to what happened to the Ark of the Covenant, and certain other sacred possessions of the Temple, it is generally assumed that they were destroyed in the burning of the Temple. Yet constant tradition asserts that it was not destroyed, and a passage in 2 Macc. ii. 4, states definitely that this was the case, and that it was rescued by Jeremiah. This passage will be fully discussed below, but for the present we ask, can we accept it as accurate evidence, apart from general tradition, that the Ark was not destroyed?

The following considerations may certainly be regarded as giving us this assurance.

First, from a merely practical point of view, we can hardly imagine the Babylonians leaving it to destruction. We have Biblical evidence that they pillaged the Temple before burning it, and removed the vessels of gold and silver, and broke up the huge brazen laver and the pillars, removing them to Babylon. Indeed, 2 Kings xxv. states that the city fell on the ninth day of the fourth month, but the Temple was not burnt until a month later, the tenth day of the fifth month (2 Kings xxv. 4, Jer. iii. 6, 12). During this month the work of demolition preparatory to burning took place, and, according to several accounts, everything of value was removed.

The Ark of the Covenant was outstandingly the most precious object in the Temple. It was the only object occupying the Holy of Holies. Its value in gold could not be estimated to-day, and even then must have been immense. The chest was overlaid inside and outside with solid gold, and the Mercy-Seat, the thickness of which is not given, surmounted by the Cherubim, was a solid slab of gold. It is unbelievable that it would have been left to destruction in the conflagration while other things of far lesser value were being removed. Apart from its intrinsic value in gold, its whole history and its sacred character could hardly have been unknown and unappreciated beyond the confines of the nation whose sacred beliefs it enshrined.

Then there is the argument of silence. While lists of the objects carried away are given, including descriptions of the breaking up of the brazen pillars and laver for transport, nothing whatever is said of this most valuable, sacred, important of all objects—the Ark of the Covenant. It was certainly not taken to Babylon or it would have been the first thing mentioned in the list of what was carried thither.

The argument of silence applies also to Babylonish records. Had the Ark been carried to Babylon it would have been regarded as the most precious of all trophies of the victory over Jerusalem. It would have found a reverenced place in one of the Temples. Babylonish records would probably have noted its arrival. It might perhaps have appeared at Belshazzar's sacrilegious feast. But no reference to it of any kind is to be found in this direction.

Finally, we must consider the sacred character of the Ark, so sacred that it was never to be seen by mortal eye, except that of the High Priest once a year. When carried in earlier days it was covered. Even in the process of covering it, no eye might look upon it, for the Veil of the Tabernacle was lowered down over it from the outside. We read of its falling into the hands of the Philistines, and of plagues attacking the inhabitants wherever it went. On being sent back on an ox-waggon the men of Beth-shemesh sacrilegiously looked within it, and 50,070 were smitten with death.

The Ark was the Divine emblem of a Divine Presence and the witness of an everlasting Divine Covenant. We to-day know what can hardly have been known then, that it was a Divine foreshadowing symbol of Christ.[1] It was the witness of promises still to come. Would God, we ask reverently, have permitted it either to suffer destruction, or fall into sacrilegious hands? The very fall of the City was a Divine fulfilment of a part of God's plans in which the Ark figured. It was a witness of things to come, some of which even to-day are awaiting fulfilment. Would Divine Providence have permitted that witness to suffer destruction before its witness was completed? It certainly was not burnt, nor was it carried to Babylon. We not only have the direct statement from Maccabees that it was rescued by Jeremiah, but, as we shall see, all the circumstances conduced to the fact, and explain the silence about it.

---

[1]   See Appendix II.

CHAPTER II

TRADITIONS REGARDING THE FATE OF THE ARK

T HERE are three traditions which claim to record what happened to the Ark, and all of them rest on foundations difficult to refute. For the present we record them in brief outline. How far they may be regarded as reliable will appear later.

1. First we have the definite information given in 2 Macc. xi. 4, which we have no reason to question. We give the passage in full.

"It was also contained in the same writing that the Prophet being warned of God, commanded the Tabernacle and the Ark to go with him, and he went forth into the mountain, where Moses climbed up, and saw the Heritage of God. And when Jeremy came thither, he found a hollow cave wherein he laid the Tabernacle, and the Ark, and the Altar of Incense, and so stopped the door.

"And some of those that followed him came to mark the way, but they could not find it.

"Which when Jeremy perceived, he blamed them, saying, As for that place it shall be unknown until the time that God gather His people again together, and receive them unto mercy.

"Then shall the Lord show them these things, and the Glory of the Lord shall appear, and the cloud also, as it was showed unto Moses, and as when Solomon desired that the place might be honourably sanctified."

We note in passing with regard to this passage that it confirms our conclusion that the Ark was not destroyed and that it was not taken to Babylon. It also assigns its rescue to the very man who, as we shall see, would be the one most likely to rescue it.

2. The second tradition is contained in a remarkable story, the main facts of which the writer is in a position to vouch for, although some of the details may need adjustment.

A year or two prior to the Great War some Biblical students discovered a cryptogram or cypher in one of the writings of the Prophet Jeremiah. This provided the information that before the burning of the Temple Jeremiah had rescued the Ark, and had taken it by an underground passage beneath the Temple, leading to a secret chamber. The cypher contained clear guidance as to where the passage and chamber lay, and how access to them could be obtained.

Permission was given by the Turkish Government for a search to be made. Under a certain Lieutenant Parker, excavation was carried out, and the passage was actually found. Unfortunately those engaged in it were incautious enough to penetrate along the passage and emerged in the early morning in the sacred precincts of the Mosque of Omar. They were seen by a woman, who reported them. The whole expedition had to go, and the members barely escaped with their lives. All further search was naturally forbidden, and soon after the war broke out.

William le Queux made the story the basis of a sensational novel entitled *The Treasure of Israel*.

3. For the third tradition, we must turn to Irish records.

Writers on this subject quote extensively from ancient Irish records, such as T*he Chronicles of Eri, The Annals of Clonmacnoise, The Annals of the Four Masters*, etc.

By co-ordinating the information contained in these works we obtain the following story:

In about the year 584 B.C. there arrived by boat at Carrickfergus in Ulster a little band, consisting of a venerable man named Ollam Fodhla, a royal princess named Tea or Tamar Tephi, and an aged companion named Simon Brug. They brought with them a sacred stone and a mysterious covered box, which was never uncovered.

The northern part of the country, now known as Ulster, was inhabited by a number of clans variously known as Scots, Milesians, and Danites, all said to have been of Israelitish descent, who had at various times arrived from overseas and settled there. They are claimed to have been mainly colonies of the maritime Tribe of Dan, who had early developed a roving disposition, and founded colonies first in Spain and Portugal, and then had sailed further on to Northern Ireland.

Ireland was ruled by Head-kings bearing the title of "Ardath," and the throne at the time was occupied by the head of one of these clans named Heremon Eochaidh I, with his seat of government at Clothair, Co. Meath, subsequently known as Tara.

Ollam Fodhla made his way thither, presented documentary credentials, which he had brought with him, and was received with highest honour.

Subsequently the marriage of Eochaidh to Tea Tephi was solemnized on the stone, Ollam Fodhla himself officiating. A national reformation based on a new code of laws introduced by Ollam Fodhla was inaugurated.

Irish tradition claims that Ollam Fodhla (Holy Prophet) was the prophet Jeremiah, Simon Brug was Baruch the scribe who figures so much in Biblical records, Tea Tephi or Tamar Tephi, was a princess, daughter of Zedekiah, and the stone was Jacob's pillow, later used in the Temple as the Coronation Seat, while finally the mysterious box was the Ark of the Covenant. On her death, in accordance with the terms of her will, the box was ultimately buried with her in the hill of Tara.

The reader will at once be sceptical of the correctness of the story and its identifications, but we ask him at present to suspend judgment until it is discussed below. It may be at once said, however, that we shall not find the box to have been the Ark of the Covenant, although it had a relationship to it, which naturally gave rise to the tradition.

Such are the three traditions which account for the mystery of the fate of the Ark of the Covenant. It would appear at first sight that they are contradictory to each other, and unless all are equally rejected, the most reliable would appear to be that which rests on the definite statement in the Book of Maccabees. It is, however, impossible to reject the story of the Sacred Cypher, since the facts of the excavations carried out in 1909-11 proved its truth, and the secret chamber and passage were actually entered.

The traditions connected with Tara may perhaps be regarded as more open to question, because, although it has never been disproved, it is in certain authoritative circles regarded as not proven.

As the story of the fate of the Ark which we shall seek to unfold does not in any way depend upon the Irish and Tara traditions, there is no necessity for the purpose we have in view to investigate them closely. They constitute an interesting corollary to our study and may be accepted or otherwise.

The account of the hiding of the Ark by Jeremiah in Mount Nebo rests, of course, on the question of the reliability of the Books of Maccabees as accurate historical records. It is given as a statement of historical fact, and as such it is difficult to account for it as a pure invention.

As regards the story of the cypher, some further information is necessary.

THE SEARCH FOR
THE ARK IN THE
HILL OF OPHEL

A very scholarly work entitled *Jerusalem Underground, Discoveries on the Hill of Ophel, 1909-1911*, a translation from the French, was published in 1911. Its author is anonymous under the initials H. V. He gives minute details, and drawings and diagrams of the excavations, and informs us that he was by the kindness of the excavators permitted access to the work at all times, from which others were rigidly excluded. The present writer has no difficulty in penetrating the anonymity of its author. He is French, and wrote in French, and is described as of the Ecole Biblique et Archéologique in Jerusalem.

The English version, we learn is "specially translated from the French for *The Field*, and fully illustrated with photographs, plans and coloured plates." London, Horace Cox, *Field* Office, Windsor House, Bream's Buildings, E.C.

A studied secrecy pervades the work. Not only is the author's name withheld, but also that of the translator. The names of all concerned in the excavation are also carefully withheld, which the English translator tells us is "for reasons which will be easily intelligible to all who are familiar with such matters." But he adds, "They will appear in due course when the completion of the Expedition's work at a subsequent date will be recorded in a final and complete volume to be published by Messrs. Constable & Co."

This work was never issued by Messrs. Constable & Co., and, on enquiry, they are able to throw no light upon the remark.

The book gives an extremely interesting account of the exploration and excavation of the network of passages round about the Virgin's Fountain in the east side of the Hill of Ophel, which forms the southern spur of Mount Moriah, now occupied by the Mosque of Omar. The special work accomplished was the clearing out of the so-called Siloam Tunnel, which connects the Virgin's Fountain with the Pool of Siloam, and in ancient times carried the water from one to the other. Ostensibly this was the object of the exploration. But the anonymous writer of the English preface reveals that this was not the true object. He describes the results of the work as ". . . successes which give promise of far more wonderful discoveries in the immediate future, for the true secret of the Hill of Ophel—it has never yet been found—has never yet so nearly been revealed as by the expedition whose work down to April 15, 1911, has been so ably described in these pages."

From this we learn that excavation work was shortly to recommence by which it was anticipated that the real objective, so nearly attained, would be consummated. The publishing of the complete story of the whole work was to be issued by Messrs. Constable & Co., after the secret object had been realised. Thus the clearing of the Siloam Tunnel, while the subject of the book, and the ostensible object of the expedition, is shown in the preface to have been only the prelude to a greater objective. But that the work was never completed nor the book published, leads us to conclude that the objective was never realized. Although this anonymous French work tells us so little yet we have no doubt we can penetrate many of its secrets. The explorers were evidently those in possession of the cypher or cryptogram referred to above, and were following the clues it contained. Who the discoverers of this cypher were we do not know. Willaim le Queux in writing his sensational novel about it, entitled *The Treasure of Israel*, clearly knew about it. His plot lies in the discovery of this cypher, which discloses the secret hiding place of the Ark of the Covenant in the Hill of Ophel. In the preface of his book he states that it is not all fiction, but that the discovery of the cypher was actually made by a well-known professor in the North of Europe. Private sources have confirmed to the author that he was a Danish professor of Hebrew. How far we may accept as accurate the details contained in the novel is uncertain. It is probable that le Queux intentionally concealed the truth in various ways, while accurately recording the main facts. He places the cypher in the Book of Ezekiel, while another account that has reached the present author places it in the Book of Deuteronomy. Ezekiel had been in exile eleven years before the destruction of Jerusalem by Nebuchadnezzar, and we see no reason why his prophecy should have contained the cypher. He was not concerned with the matter. Less probable still is the Book of Deuteronomy, for it assumes the modernist claim that the Pentateuch dates from postexilic times, which we do not admit.

The more likely source of the cypher is one of the works of the Prophet Jeremiah, who was himself chief actor, and wrote both his prophecy and Lamentations at the time.

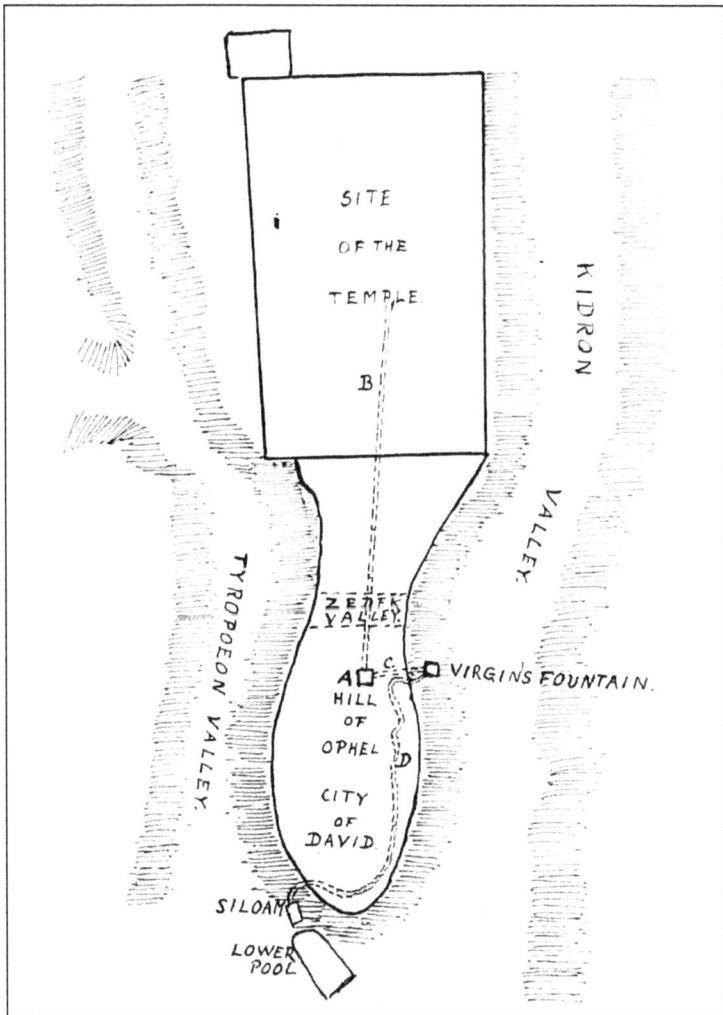

ENLARGED MAP OF THE HILL OF OPHEL

*showing the position of the Virgin's Fountain, the Siloam
Tunnel (D), and probable position of the Secret Chamber (C)*

It was from a reliable source that the present writer learnt that the expedition was known as the Parker expedition, and was led by a Lieutenant Parker. The same source supplied the information recorded above, that the chamber was actually found as indicated by the cypher, and that the explorers penetrated up the passage, emerging under the Mosque of Omar, with the result that they were seen and had to fly for their lives. This would account for the fact that the contemplated book was never issued. The Ark was not found, the chamber was empty.

THE SILOAM TUNNEL

Copyright photograph of the American Colony, Jerusalem

CHAPTER IV

LOCATION OF THE FIRST HIDING PLACE OF THE ARK

No one would regard as reliable information drawn from a novel, however much it might claim to be based on historical fact, and especially a novel of the type and character of those by William le Queux. That many of his works were erected on a substratum of fact and truth is readily admitted, but since his purpose was usually that of the popular sensational press, it is difficult to extract truth and fact from mere journalistic padding.

In referring to his novel, the present author starts with the ground-work of information obtained from the reliable source referred to above, and the novel only assists him to check off this information and to illuminate it. He relies on no information from the novel, which is not otherwise corroborated.

In his novel, William le Queux gives important information regarding this secret hiding place of the Ark, and whatever reliability may be placed upon other parts of the information contained in his story, this may obviously be regarded as accurate. There would be no purpose in inventing it on his part.

He tells us that the Ark and other precious relics were "*concealed beneath the earth in a dry-room in connection with which is a series of water tunnels.*"

The italics are William le Queux's, and he puts them in inverted commas, thus showing that he is directly quoting from a document containing his information. He is not inventing, and we may add that his statement is otherwise corroborated.

He goes on to tell us that the secret chamber had "three entrances, one of which is impossible as it is inaccessible, being closed up by masonry in a labyrinth of caves; the second is also too difficult. But the third is accessible by draining the water, and will not present much difficulty."

This part is not in italics, but is obviously accurate information from the same document.

By applying this information to that disclosed in *Underground Jerusalem*, and the 1909-11 research work, whose confessed object was a secret of the highest importance, we are left in no doubt as to the location of, and access to, this secret chamber.

The chamber lay in the Hill of Ophel behind the Virgin's Fountain. The first entrance, which was "inaccessible being closed by masonry in a labyrinth of caves," was the passage leading up to the Temple hill. It ended in the labyrinth of chambers which lay under the Temple, and still lie under the Mosque of Omar. Any attempt to enter the secret chamber from under the Mosque of Omar down this passage, along which the Ark was actually carried by Jeremiah, was quite impossible to the Parker explorers. The Mosque authorities would never have permitted it, and in any case, its entrance lay concealed behind some unknown part of the massive masonry that lines the underground chambers and caves under the Mosque.

"The second entrance was also too difficult." This we surmise was probably the Siloam Tunnel, the excavation of which was the ostensible object of the expedition. There was obviously a branch connection between the Siloam Tunnel and the secret chamber.

"The third entrance is accessible by draining the water, and will not present much difficulty." Here we have the key to the work carried out, by the Parker expedition. The drawings and diagrams in *Underground Jerusalem* show a number of rocky cisterns filled with water at the Virgin's Fountain. Very little of this water could at the time get away down the Siloam Tunnel to the Pool of Siloam. Covered by water in one of these cisterns was the entrance of a short tunnel leading straight into the secret chamber. The first work to be carried out, therefore, was to clear the Siloam Tunnel so that the water could flow properly down its accustomed channel, and some of the cisterns could be emptied. This was done and the entrance evidently was found. On April 15, 1911, having completed this work and found the entrance, the party temporarily ceased work during the hot months. The secret objective of the expedition was thus, as stated in the translator's preface, on the verge of being realized. So certain were they of success that the research party made all preparations for entrance into the chamber, and arrangements for publishing the great discovery, which they expected to make in it.

Later, probably in the early autumn, the work was resumed, the chamber actually entered, and the explorers penetrated up the passage, leading to the chambers under the Mosque, down which Jeremiah had carried the Ark. Here, as stated above, they unwisely emerged and were seen, and the whole expedition had to leave the country.

Why was the Ark not found? Why was the chamber empty?

William le Queux gives what purports to be another quotation from the cypher. It is again in italics and in quotation marks. It runs: "*The tablets shall remain in their hiding-place till the arrival of the Messiah, who alone may open their place of concealment, in order that He may furnish proof of the faith, and if necessary the treasure shall provide a war fund when the Messiah conquers the world, and establishes His residence in Jerusalem."*

We note that the first part of this statement conforms closely with the statement in 2 Macc. ii, but the latter part can hardly be otherwise than spurious, as no Bible prophecies ever predict the Messiah waging an earthly war with earthly material to gain His Kingdom.

We thus have what may be regarded as two definite accounts of the fate of the Ark of the Covenant—that contained in the second book of Maccabees, that Jeremiah hid it in a cave in Mount Nebo, and that contained in the story of the secret cypher. There is also the third tradition which emanates from Ireland, and associates its fate with the Hill of Tara.

Are these accounts necessarily contradictory?

CHAPTER V

THE STORY OF THE RESCUE OF THE ARK

The Story Unfolded

THE prophecy of Jeremiah provides us with data which, when examined closely, enable us to arrive at a complete explanation of, and harmony between, the three traditions, and a convincing consecutive story of what happened.

Jeremiah lived during the closing stages of the history of the Kingdom of Judah, during which the country was a buffer state between the two powerful rival Kingdoms of Babylon and Egypt. The policy which Jeremiah consistently urged was friendship with Babylon, a policy which was most unpopular and continually rejected by both king and people. His advice fell upon deaf ears, but his constant warnings proved true when a Babylonish army, under Nebuchadnezzar; invaded the land and captured Jerusalem. King Jehoiachin and a number of captives were taken to Babylon. The Temple was partially pillaged, but left otherwise undamaged. Zedekiah, a son of Josiah, was placed on the throne as a vassal of Babylon.

As was to be expected, Jeremiah was regarded with great disfavour by the people, who associated the disasters of their country with him, since he had predicted them. He appears, however, to have been unmolested in the city and continued to utter his warnings against friendship with Egypt, and hostility towards Babylon. His warnings continued to fall upon deaf ears. Popular opinion still urged friendship with Egypt, and the weak king at length yielded to the popular urge, and finally openly threw off the Babylonish yoke. Another Babylonish invasion resulted, and Jerusalem was besieged by an army under the command of Nebuzaradan.

After the city had been invested for some considerable time, an Egyptian army under Pharaoh Hophra advanced to its relief. The siege was for a time raised by the Babylonish army in order to repel the Egyptian relief force, which was completely defeated and driven back to Egypt.

During the respite occasioned by the raising of the siege, Jeremiah attempted to retire from the city into Benjamin. He was, however, arrested at the gate, and falsely accused of high treason by attempting to join the Babylonians. He was beaten and condemned to close and harsh imprisonment at the hands of Jonathan the scribe (Jer. xxxvii. 11-16).

The guilty conscience of the king pricked him, and, on hearing of the harsh treatment meted out to

Jeremiah, he "asked him secretly in his own house, and said, Is there any word from the Lord?" Jeremiah protested against his imprisonment and the cruelties perpetrated upon him, and Zedekiah committed him to milder confinement in the court of the prison (Jer. xxxvii. 16-21).

The malignity of the princes would not brook this, and they accused him before the King of causing disaffection on the part of the people and weakening their resistance to Babylon by his utterances. They demanded his death. The King again weakly yielded to their importunities, and he was delivered into their hands. He was cast into a foul pit in the prison, into which he was lowered by cords.

An official of the royal palace, Ebed-melech the Ethiopian, however, had the temerity to plead for him before the King, who permitted him to rescue Jeremiah with the aid of thirty men.

Jeremiah was now restored to mild confinement in the court of the prison, where he remained until the end of the siege.

The siege was renewed, and apparently lasted some two years. At length a breach was made on the north side. Zedekiah secretly evacuated the city with the flower of his army and his nobles by the "gate between the two walls." This gate lay on the south side of the city, somewhere where the deep Tyropoean Valley, Kedron

Valley, and Valley of Hinnom all converge. The chief enemy attacks would be from the north and the west, where the ground was more on a level with the city walls, but on this south side the enemy could not closely beset the city, and escape was thus possible. Zedekiah fled down the valley towards Jericho. His flight was betrayed, and he was pursued and captured at Jericho. His fate is recorded. He was taken before Nebuchadnezzar at his headquarters at Riblah. His sons were slain before his eyes, and his own eyes were put out, and he was transported a life prisoner to Babylon.

Jeremiah was still in the court of the prison when the city fell (Jer. xxxviii. 28), and was at once kindly received by Nebuzaradan, who had received the following remarkable instructions from Nebuchadnezzar regarding him.

"Take him, and look well to him, and do him no harm; but do unto him even as he shall say unto thee" (Jer. xxxix. 12).

Nebuchadnezzar was clearly aware of the attitude which Jeremiah had consistently adopted of friendship to Babylon, and of the sufferings he had in consequence endured. We must recall the fact that in earlier days Jehoiakim had been a vassal of Nebuchadnezzar, and had then rebelled. This had resulted in the first capture of Jerusalem by Nebuchadnezzar. Jeremiah was prophecying in those days and had intercourse with the Babylonish authorities when in the city. He must have been known to them as an outstanding figure, and their friend.

Before the departure of the Babylonish army, after the burning of the Temple, the grandson of an old courtier of the reign of Josiah, named Gedaliah, was appointed governor of the land, devastated and depopulated except for the poor, who were suffered to remain to till the soil. Jeremiah was given the opportunity of going to Babylon, where honours were awaiting him. He elected, however, to join Gedaliah, and assist him with the government which he set up at Mizpah (Jer. xl. 1-6).

We have noted above that Nebuzaradan had received instructions not only to treat Jeremiah kindly, but to concede any requests he might make. We are not specifically told in what these requests consisted, and many reasons may be deduced for his not giving them, but subsequent events do not leave us in any doubt as to their nature. They seem to have been three in number. First, we find "the King's daughters" subsequently under his guardianship. They are with Gedaliah at Mizpah (Jer. xli. 10, and xliii. 6). It is obvious that this formed his first request. He would point out that they were innocent and helpless. Their brothers had been put to death. Their father, blinded, was being taken to Babylon. It was a humane request which could be granted without hesitation.

The second request, which subsequent events suggest, if ancient traditions are to be relied upon, was that he might take possession from the Temple of the Coronation stone, which is claimed to have been none other than Jacob's pillow of Bethel.[1] That this stone had been held as a national heirloom, and had been set up as a Coronation dais in the Temple, and eventually found its way to Westminster, there known as the Stone of Scone, is a tradition mentioned in official Westminster guides. These traditions and those as to its arrival in Ireland have already been mentioned, and will be discussed below.

One thing, however, may be said; if the many traditions regarding this stone have any truth in them, then the request to be allowed to secure it was both natural and appropriate. The princesses, by tradition two in number, placed under his guardianship, were the survivors of the royal family.

The stone was the royal heirloom on which all their ancestors had apparently been enthroned since David. Valueless in itself, it would be regarded by Nebuzaradan as only of sentimental value to them. Why should they not have it? If, indeed, it was Jacob's pillow, to Jeremiah it possessed a sacred character as a witness to Covenant promises and prophecies still to be realized, and in which the two princesses were to take their part.

As a third request we are justified in concluding that Jeremiah asked for possession of the Ark of the Covenant, the Altar of Incense, and other sacred objects in the Temple. The willing surrender of so valuable an object as the Ark of the Covenant by Nebuzaradan is easily explicable. Jeremiah would tell him of its past history, which had established not only its highly sacred character, but the extreme danger of its possession in alien hands. It had brought plagues wherever it had been taken while in Philistine hands, even the Israelite men of Beth-shemesh had been smitten with death to the number of 50,070 for the sacrilege of looking into it. Nebuzaradan had himself acknowledged that his conquest of the city had been in fulfilment of the prophecies of Jeremiah, and with the consent of the God of Judah whose prophet he was (Jer. xl. 1-4). The Ark of the Covenant was the sacred emblem of that God, and must be preserved in the safe-keeping of His Prophet. Any attempt on the part of Babylon to remove it would be fraught with danger and disaster.

The request would, therefore, be conceded, and its removal would be carried out under the direct protection of Nebuzaradan.

The tradition that Jeremiah removed it through an underground passage to a secret chamber must be accepted as a fact. The discovery of the cypher, which led to the actual discovery of the chamber and passage is a fact, and provides information as to the natural line of action which we should expect to find followed.

If we cannot reject the evidences and inferences that Jeremiah did in fact rescue the Ark, some explanation as to how he was enabled to do so is necessary. Nebuchadnezzar's command to Nebuzaradan to honour any specific request on the part of Jeremiah supplies us with a complete explanation.

The Temple hill is honeycombed with underground passages and chambers. Even to-day some of these are known to exist, and are guarded with utmost secrecy on the part of the Mohammedan owners of the Mosque of Omar. The description of the excavation of the Siloam Tunnel given in *Underground Jerusalem* reveals that other tunnels exist, running from the Virgin's Fountain. The so-called Solomon's stables are open to visitors, and other passages have been entered by explorers.

The only way in which the safety of the Ark could be immediately secured was by its removal to some such underground chamber. To have transported it elsewhere above ground would at the time have been impossible, and endangered its future security.

It would be more than probable that in thus removing it Jeremiah, knowing that the Temple would be burnt, and the city utterly destroyed, would leave some clue as to where it had been concealed, and there is nothing improbable about his doing so by means of a cypher in some work he was then writing.

His mind would ever be fixed upon his own prediction that in seventy years time the people would return, and the city and Temple would be rebuilt. What the immediate future would bring forth was uncertain. He himself might not survive. It was, therefore, essential that a clue to the immediate hiding place of the Ark must be preserved, and forthcoming when the Temple would be rebuilt. There need be no reasonable doubt but that the Ark was thus rescued by Jeremiah.

The Second Removal of the Ark

But events were to bring it about that this was not to be the final resting-place of the Ark.

The new governor of Palestine, Gedaliah, set up a government at Mizpah, and here Jeremiah repaired with the two daughters of Zedekiah. The statement in the second book of Maccabees cannot be an invention. It is stated to have been recorded in records. It is not, therefore, a mere oral tradition quoted by the writer of the books of Maccabees, but is taken from the written records from which he is compiling his works. The short period of quiet which followed the departure of the Babylonish army with its host of captives provided Jeremiah with the opportunity to remove the Ark to greater safety, and this he appears to have done under Divine instructions. In fact, we have a distinct Bible implication that he was absent for a time from Mizpah, after placing the daughters of Zedekiah in the care of the governor, Gedaliah. The circumstances were as follows:

The Assassination of Gedaliah

The news of the appointment of Gedaliah as governor by Babylon, and his establishment of a seat of government at Mizpah soon spread among the bordering nations of Moab, Ammon, and Edom, whither many of the Jews had fled during the invasion. These returned and rallied to the support of Gedaliah. Among them came a traitor named Ishmael, a member of the royal family, who had been a refugee in the Court of Baalis, King of Ammon. This man hatched a plot to assassinate Gedaliah. Warning of the plot was given by Johanan, who declared that Ishmael was the tool of the King of Ammon, but the warning was disregarded.

Gedaliah entertained him and ten companions at a meal, and was foully murdered and all with him. This horrible crime was followed by a further crime in the murder of a band of seventy men who arrived at Mizpah on a visit two days later.

Ishmael next laid his hands on the two daughters of Zedekiah, and those who had been spared in the massacre, and set out to return to Ammon. They were, however, overtaken at Gibeon by Johanan and his followers to whom news of the crime had been conveyed. Ishmael with eight of his followers escaped, but all the prisoners, including the royal princesses, were rescued. Johanan now assumed the governorship in the place of the murdered Gedaliah.

It is not difficult to find a true motive for this crime. Ishmael, as a member of the royal family was evidently aspiring to the throne of his deposed relative Zedekiah.

His claim to the throne would be greatly strengthened by marriage with one of the king's daughters. Being promised the support of the King of Ammon he, therefore, perpetrated this crime largely to gain possession of the persons of the two royal princesses.

What is, however, significant is that, while we find Jeremiah residing at Mizpah just before the crime, his name is nowhere mentioned during the events that followed. Had he been present at the time he would undoubtedly have been one of the victims. He was not taken along with the daughters of Zedekiah. He, too, would certainly have added his warning to that of Johanan. It is clear that when the crime was perpetrated, he was temporarily absent. (Jeremiah xl, xli). Where was he?

The country was devastated and its cities destroyed; only a mere handful of poverty-stricken people remained scattered here and there. We may depict Jeremiah leaving Mizpah with a small band of intimates, and visiting the blackened ruins of Jerusalem. Here he penetrates into the secret passage and chamber, and quietly removes the Ark. They reverently carry it away, across the Jordan to the mountains of Gilead and hide it in the cave in Mount Nebo, the mount from which Moses was permitted to view the Promised Land before his death. The entrance was carefully concealed.

The fact, however, was not concealed, for, as stated, we read that subsequently attempts were made to find it in vain. Jeremiah explains their failure by the remarkable statement, "As for the place, it shall be unknown until the time that God gather His people again together and receive them unto mercy. Then shall the Lord shew them these things, and the glory of the Lord shall appear."

The hiding-place of the Ark is to be disclosed in God's own time. But can we estimate how, or when?

CHAPTER VI

THE SECRET OF NEHEMIAH'S MIDNIGHT RAMBLE

I NDIRECT inferential confirmation of the hiding of the Ark by Jeremiah may perhaps be found in an incident which Nehemiah records about himself in Chapter ii, 11-16 of his book.

Nehemiah has been given leave of absence from the Court of the King of Persia to enable him to proceed to Jerusalem for the purpose of rebuilding the walls.

It is generally stated by most commentators that this took place 14 years after 50,000 Jews had returned under Ezra by decree of Cyrus and had rebuilt the Temple. Yet in two works by "Lumen," entitled *The Master of Magicians*,[2] and *The Prince of Judah*, convincing reasons are put forward for placing his visit much earlier. "Lumen" places the visit during the seven years illness or madness of Nebuchadnezzar during which

---

[2]   These two works appeared in 1905 and 1906, published by Messrs. Elliot Stock, but are now out of print.

his brother-in-law the King of Persia controlled the Babylonian Empire. Apart from the historical evidences with which he supports this view, he shows from the opening verses of the Book of Nehemiah that Jerusalem was at the time a complete ruin, and inhabited only by some of the poor remnant left behind by Nebuchadnezzar after the destruction of the city in 584 B.C.

We recall how after the murder of Gedaliah his friend Johanan had for a time assumed the governorship, but he had migrated to Egypt taking Jeremiah with him. Some twenty years had since elapsed, and a miserable body of Jews had gradually settled again in the ruined city, but no attempt had been made to rebuild it.

Hanani, a brother of Nehemiah, visits him at Shushan the Palace in Persia, and his visit to Jerusalem resulted. "Lumen" shows that the Queen whom Nehemiah mentions was probably Esther, and doubtless her influence gained him permission to go.

The more one studies the arguments put forward by "Lumen" for this early date for the visit of Nehemiah before the return under Ezra, the more convincing do they appear. Be this as it may, he came to Jerusalem at a time of a great national depression, to re-build the walls.

Arriving at the city, he first spends three days evidently to make a thorough examination of the condition of the ruined walls, and formulate his plans for organizing the rebuilding of them. Then occurs the incident referred to. It consisted of a secret midnight reconnoitre outside the south wall of the city. He several times emphasizes the secrecy of his investigation. "I, and some few men with me: neither told I any man what God had put into my heart to do at Jerusalem, neither was there any beast with me save the beast that I rode upon." Again, "and the rulers knew not whither I went, or what I did, neither had I as yet told it to the Jews, nor to the priests, nor to the nobles, nor to the rulers, nor to the rest that did work." There was thus some secret purpose behind this midnight ramble, known only to himself, so secret that although several men accompanied him he did not even take them into his confidence. He next tells us actually what he did. Passing out of the Valley Gate, he made his way along the ruins of the south-east wall as far as the "Dragon's Well," passing in turn the Dung Gate, the Fountain Gate, and the King's Pool.

Professor MacAlister, in his *A Century of Excavation in Palestine*, summarizes the conclusions of experts as to the identity of these gates, the remains of both of which were actually found by Bliss.

The ancient city of Jerusalem extended much further south than the present city. The Hill of Ophel formed a spur of the Temple Hill enclosed in walls and entirely separated from the main southern part of the city by the deep Tyropoean Valley. It is now well established that the Hill of Ophel was the ancient City of David.

MAP OF ANCIENT JERUSALEM

Illustrating Nehemiah's midnight ramble

The Valley Gate was the southernmost gate of the main part of the city. The southern wall crossed the Tyropoean Valley straight to the Pool of Siloam. Between the Valley Gate and the Pool of Siloam lay the two gates identified by Bliss, the Dung Gate and the Fountain Gate. The King's Pool was the lower part of the Pool of Siloam, and the Fountain Gate was that leading to it near the south end of the Hill of Ophel. Nehemiah passed out of the Valley Gate, turned east, passing along the ruined wall down into the Tyropoean Valley, past these two gates, to the Pool of Siloam. Here he turned north along the Kedron as far as the Dragon's Well, which must have been the Virgin's Fountain. At this point he retraced his steps, and we may conclude that the south end of the Siloam Tunnel and the Virgin's Fountain were the objectives of his excursion. Ostensibly he was merely inspecting this section of the wall, but apart from the fact that he tells us some secret motive prompted the expedition, it is obvious that the mere observation of this small section of the city wall could have been better carried out in daylight, and could not have been the true object of the ramble.

We can hardly doubt, but that he was investigating two of the three entrances to the secret chamber in which Jeremiah had first hidden the Ark. The ostensible object of merely examining this short section of the city wall would serve as a blind to those who accompanied him.

His remark about having told no one may, of course, imply that he had as yet withheld the general purpose of his visit, but as regards this ramble it is clear from what he says that a special secret purpose lay behind it.

We have already described how the research work carried out in 1909-11, and described in H.V.'s *Underground Jerusalem*, consisted in the excavation of the Virgin's Fountain, and the tunnel which runs down from it to the Pool of Siloam. Other tunnels as yet unexplored run in behind the Virgin's Fountain, one of which gave access to the secret hiding place of the Ark, and thence up to the area beneath the Temple. We can hardly doubt but that Nehemiah,

living at Shushan the Palace in Persia, had the fullest information regarding all that had happened at the time of the destruction of Babylon. "Lumen" suggests that he had been sent by the Court of Babylon to the Court of Persia when Nebuchadnezzar became ill. It is quite probable that Jeremiah's writings were known to him. He was a member of the royal family and we cannot doubt but that Jeremiah was in constant communication with him, and reporting all events at Jerusalem. He would naturally be the one to whom Jeremiah would confide his secrets. Ezekiel had been in Babylon, and they may have discussed matters, and the future of their race. If the cypher was contained in the book of Ezekiel, as William le Queux tells us, then Ezekiel himself may have informed Nehemiah of the secret hiding-place of the Ark. But, as stated, we believe that Jeremiah himself communicated his information. Its second and secret removal to Mount Nebo by Jeremiah would hardly be known. This had been carried out just prior to Jeremiah's departure for Egypt, whence he sailed for Spain and Britain, and the very fact that 2 Macc. ii. quotes him as saying that its hiding place was to be preserved by God, implies that he disclosed it to no one. We conclude, therefore, that he wrote to Nehemiah a full account of the destruction of the city and burning of the Temple, and of his rescue of the Ark, and how he placed it in its first hiding place, but did not at a later date write of his subsequent removal of it to Nebo, which he had been divinely warned was to remain secret.

Whatever was the date of this visit of Nehemiah, it is evident from the list of names he gives of those who assisted him to build the walls that a considerable and influential number of Jews had drifted back to the ruined city.

Hanani his brother, who had come from Jerusalem, may have known of the first hiding of the Ark in Ophel. By whatever means Nehemiah had learnt of the fact, there can be little doubt but that this was the secret of his midnight ramble. His purpose in coming to Jerusalem was to take the Ark out of its secret hiding place, as he thought in Mount Ophel, and thus use it to inspire the whole nation in reestablishing themselves in Jerusalem.

He passes out of the Valley Gate, turns east, and skirts along the ruined wall until he reaches the Pool of Siloam. This is silted up with rubble, and the flow of water down the tunnel is impeded. It is clear that access to the secret chamber, in which he thinks the Ark is still hidden, is impossible from this end of the Siloam tunnel. He leaves his mule, and passes up the east wall of Ophel along the Kedron Brook as far as the Virgin's Fountain. Here the cisterns are also all choked, and it is obvious that a good deal must be done before the short tunnel leading from here to the secret chamber can be penetrated. This will perhaps be the easiest way of entering the chamber. Having made his observations he retraces his steps, and observes strict silence.

The work of rebuilding the walls must first be completed, and then, when the city is safely enclosed he will be in a position to withdraw the Ark from its secret hiding-place, either by way of Siloam or the Virgin's Fountain, and Jerusalem will once more obtain something of its ancient glory.

One thing is clear, Nehemiah found the two entrances from the Virgin's Fountain and the Siloam

Tunnel were too much choked to penetrate. The great secret must not, of course, be disclosed until the great work of rebuilding the walls of Jerusalem was complete. He may have intended at this stage merely to make a secret entry into this chamber to make sure the Ark was there. He quite probably subsequently did go down the passage from the Temple, only to find it empty. Whether he subsequently found out about its second removal by Jeremiah to Mount Nebo, of course we do not know.

IRISH TRADITIONS

A s recorded above the Irish records inform us that Ollam Fodhla, whom many identify with Jeremiah, brought with him a mysterious covered box, which was ultimately buried with Tamar Tephi in the hill of Tara.

We have traced the Ark to Mount Nebo, and have noted Jeremiah's prediction that here it was to remain in its secret hiding-place until God reveals it. The box cannot, therefore, have been the Ark of the Covenant. In consequence some readers may feel that any further consideration of Irish records and the box is irrelevant to our purpose.

Yet our story may prove to be incomplete if there is truth in the Irish traditions.

Assuming for the present that Ollam Fodhla was Jeremiah, Simon Brug was Baruch the scribe, Tamar Tephi a daughter of Zedekiah, and the stone was Jacob's pillow, what then was the box? We suggest it was the case in which Jeremiah preserved all his sacred documents. These would include the MSS. of his prophetic writings, the credentials which he brought with him, including proofs of the identities of the party, and finally, the full description of the place of hiding of the Ark of the Covenant. The contents of this box were to be the key to the future, and the proof of the Davidic descent of Tamar Tephi, and of the long line of kingly descendants, which have since sprung from her, reaching right down to King George VI.

In Jeremiah Chapter xxxii. we have recorded how Jeremiah was commanded to purchase a field, as an act of faith in the ultimate fulfilment of the Divine Promises, and the ultimate restoration of the nation. The purchase deeds were carefully stored in an earthen vessel under the seal, "That they may continue many days." We suggest that this vessel may also have had a place in the box. It is possible also that some relic of the Tabernacle which was stored in the Temple, or of the Temple itself, preserved in the box would be one of the best possible proofs of his identity. 2 Macc. ii. informs us that relics of the 'Tabernacle were deposited with the Ark in Mount Nebo.

Such we believe to have been the contents of the sacred box. The grave of Tamar Tephi would be the natural and appropriate hiding-place for such a box, if Providence ruled that the truth was not to be known until God willed it. Jeremiah declared this to be so.

But how far can we rely on the accuracy of these Irish traditions?

To establish this it is necessary first to account for the departure of Jeremiah from Palestine.

After concealing the Ark in Mount Nebo we find Jeremiah at Chimham near Bethlehem, the new seat of government set up by Johanan. It is to be noted that between the murder of Gedaliah at Mizpah and the setting up of this new seat of government by his successor Johanan, at Chimham, near Bethlehem, where Jeremiah reappears, there is complete silence as to his movements in the Biblical records. This confirms our conclusion that it was during this interval that his second removal of the Ark to Mount Nebo took place.

So deplorable had the condition of affairs become that a decision was taken by Johanan and his followers to migrate to Egypt. Jeremiah strongly protested against this course, and warned Johanan that Babylon was about to attack Egypt, and they would be no more safe there than in Palestine. His warnings were rejected, and he was forced against his will to accompany them. The party settled in Tarpanhes in Egypt. (Jer. XLIII.)

Here Biblical records cease, and we must rely upon profane. We give them without comment or attempting to establish their accuracy.

It is a well-established fact that the maritime tribe of Dan had from the earliest times developed a roving disposition. They became great mariners, and their ships, known as ships of Tarshish, sailed to many coastal towns all round the Mediterranean.[3]

At first they formed many distant colonies in Spain and Portugal, but eventually travelled right round into the Atlantic and on to Northern Ireland. Here, also, a number of colonies were established. These colonists were variously known as Iberians, Scots, Milesians, and Danites. They maintained a regular trade and intercourse with the mother country of Palestine. The story of these far distant Israelitish and mainly Danite colonies is too large a subject to be here dealt with, but many works have been written on the subject.

Many place names still attest the fact. Two large collections of MSS. and documents relating to the Spanish and Portuguese Israelitish colonies are known to have existed belonging to Don Gil Mendez, of Miranda del Ebro and Santander, and to a gentleman named Enriquez, but one was wantonly destroyed by the Carlist General Iturralde, in 1838, and the other collection by another, General Leon, in 1838 or 1839.

---

[3] The location of Tarshish has always been a subject of conjecture. It is generally identified with Tartessus in Spain, a great emporium of Phoenician trade. Trade ships from Syria to this port were known as ships of Tarshish. But in process of time the expression came to be attached to all larger vessels, which we should describe to-day as "Ocean-going" vessels, as distinct fromsmaller coastalvessels.

These various colonies were formed into clans, and ruled by their own Chieftains.

Knowing well that Egypt would be overrun by Babylonish armies, Jeremiah determined to leave Tarpanhes before it was too late, and he set sail for Spain taking with him his wards, the two daughters of Zedekiah, and his scribe Baruch, and the stone, and the box.

Here it appears that one of the princesses married a Spanish Danite chieftain, but Jeremiah pushed on to the more distant settlements of Northern Ireland, now known as Ulster.

The Irish traditions of the arrival of Ollam Fodhla have been given above, and the vital question remains, was Ollam Fodhla Jeremiah?

The following considerations have an important bearing upon the subject.

Irish traditions emphatically assert the fact, and "Jerry" or Jeremiah is one of the most popular of Irish names. The name Ollam Fodhla is Irish, and means "Holy Prophet," which reflects his character. It appears to have been a title borne by religious teachers and law-givers.

Two places claim to have his grave. The best authenticated is Old Castle, to the west of Tara, where a huge mound of stones is said still to mark the spot. Here also is a large, curiously cut stone claimed to have been his judicial seat.

Traditions state that he inaugurated a national reformation, and instituted a new code of laws. In the famous Four Courts of Dublin, destroyed some years ago in a riot, were large medallions round the roof giving portraits of the world's famous law-givers. They included Solon, Alfred, Confucius, Moses, and—Ollam Fodhla. The change of the name of the seat of government from Clothair to Tara suggests the Hebrew word *torah*, the law.

Tamar is, of course, a Jewish name, and occurs in Hebrew pedigrees. Tea and Tephi are Irish and appear to mean "Beautiful wanderer."

With regard to the stone, the remarkable subsequent history attached to it shows that on its arrival it was received with the highest reverence suggesting some sacred past history, and the fact that Ollam Fodhla had brought it from afar supports this suggestion.

With regard to the box, although certain Irish tradition asserts that it was actually the Ark, if at the time it was known to contain sacred clues as to the fate of the Ark, it would be perfectly natural that in after years the tradition would arise that it actually was the Ark.

One final closing point needs some explanation. The passage in the second book of Maccabees states Jeremiah to have declared that the Ark would remain concealed in Mount Nebo until "God gather together again His people and receive them unto mercy."

The whole trend of Bible prophecy is to the effect that the whole Israelite race is to see a national restoration to their own land of Palestine, and an ultimate recognition of Christ as their Messiah.

It is a remarkable fact that the actual identity of Mount Nebo is unknown. This is the more remarkable because the Bible seems so clearly to indicate its position. It is described as the summit of Mount Pisgah, in the Land of Moab, facing Jericho. Its position is further indicated by the ravine in which Moses was buried, apparently part of the mountain itself. "The ravine in the Land of Moab facing Beth-Peor." Pisgah is well known yet no one has been able to identify Nebo. Pisgah's summit is an extensive mountain plateau with several peaks, any one of which might be Nebo.

CHAPTER VIII

THE TRADITIONAL STORY OF THE CORONATION STONE

Is it, as Tradition asserts, Jacob's Pillow at Bethel?

T HE tradition has subsisted from time imme-
morial, and is quoted in official guides, that the
Stone of Scone, set in the Coronation chair, is none
other than that on which the head of Jacob rested when
he dreamed of the ladder with angels ascending, and descending upon it.

Is it but an idle fable? Traditions do not spring from
nothing, and this one is at least worthy of impartial
examination.

From Bethel to Westminster is a long distance both
as regards time and space, and any attempt to connect
the two involves of necessity the reconstruction of a
consecutive, feasible story. There is no doubt but that
such a story can be traced, and when examined few will
fail to admit that the links prove to be more substan-
tial than the strangeness of the tradition would suggest.

The story may be likened to an arch, the left-hand span of which, starting at Bethel, carries us through Biblical history upward to the destruction of Jerusalem in *circa* 584 B.C., by Nebuchadnezzar. The right-hand span of the arch begins at Westminster, reaching backwards to Tara in Ireland, approximately at the same date, 584 B.C. The keystone is the central part of the story from Jerusalem to Ireland at about that date. The left-hand span from Bethel onwards to Jerusalem at its destruction in 584 rests on Biblical records, and a feasible story may be traced. The right-hand span from Westminster back to Ireland is more modern history. The keystone which connects Jerusalem with Tara in Ireland rests on ancient tradition and Irish records, which need careful examination.

From Westminster back to Ireland

The more modern part of the story from Westminster back to Ireland rests on well-authenticated historical documents giving than the strangeness of the tradition would suggest.

The story may be likened to an arch, the left-hand span of which, starting at Bethel, carries us through Biblical history upward to the destruction of Jerusalem in *circa* 584 B.C., by Nebuchadnezzar. The right-hand span of the arch begins at Westminster, reaching backwards to Tara in Ireland, approximately at the same date, 584 B.C. The keystone is the central part of the story from Jerusalem to Ireland at about that date. The left-hand span from Bethel onwards to Jerusalem at its destruction in 584 rests on Biblical records, and a feasible story may be traced. The right-hand span from Westminster back to Ireland is more modern history. The keystone which connects Jerusalem with Tara in Ireland rests on ancient tradition and Irish records, which need careful examination.

From Westminster back to Ireland

The more modern part of the story from Westminster back to Ireland rests on well-authenticated historical documents giving successively Irish, Scottish, and English records, and may be regarded as practically undisputed. Writers on the subject, quoting from such works as *The Chronicles of Eri, The Annals of the Four Masters, The Annals of Clonmacnoise*, etc., locate the stone originally at Tara, Co. Meath, Ireland. Naturally such early records as these are uncertain as to dates, but from Dr. Lynch's *Cambrensis Eversus*, published in Latin in 1662, and translated in 1848, the year *circa* 584 B.C., may be taken as the Tara starting date.

KING EDWARD'S CHAIR

Containing the Coronation Stone of Scone

The coronation of Heremon Eochaidh I on a "stone wonderful" at about this date is told in *The Chronicles of Eri*. Recorded movements of the stone were from Tara to Dunstaffnage in Scotland in *circa* A.D. 498,[4] thence to the monstery of Iona to the care of St. Columba in 565. In A.D. 836 we find it removed to Scone, near Perth, whence it was taken to Westminster by Edward I.

Ancient genealogies (*The Four Masters, The Anglo-Saxon Chronicle*, Glover, Pineda, Keating, Grimaldi, etc.), give us the names of the 54 Ardaths or Head-Kings of Ireland crowned upon the stone at Tara. At Dunstaffnage and Jona fourteen kings of Argyle, and at Scone a long list of kings of United Scotland used it at their coronations. Since Edward I every British Sovereign has been crowned upon it at Westminster.[5]

The stone during all this period was known as "the Lial Fail" or "Stone of Destiny." Thus the later part of the story of the stone from Tara to Westminster is clear, and may be regarded as practically unchallenged, covering a period from about 584 B.C. to the present date.

---

[4] See *The Times Coronation Supplement*, May 11, 1937, which gives us this as the date of Fergus the first, King of Argyle, who transported the stone from Tara to Dunstaffnage.

[5] It is frequently asserted that Mary Tudor preferred to use a chair specially sent by the Pope for the occasion. This appears to be incorrect. She seems to have used both.

From Bethel to the Destruction of Jerusalem

Turning next to the early part of the story, namely that from Bethel to the destruction of Jerusalem in 584 B.C., here, again, it is possible to reconstruct a feasible story from Biblical records. Parts of it may be regarded as more open to question owing to differing interpretations of Scripture, than the more modern history of the stone, but at least Bible inferences both direct and indirect.in support of it may be cited.

We give it as it stands. Close discussion upon it is beyond our scope. The story of the stone begins with the account of how Jacob sets out on his journey for Mesopotamia, and reaches Luz or Bethel at nightfall. He lies down to sleep in the open, resting his head on a stone by way of a pillow. In his dream he sees the vision of the ladder, with angels ascending and descending upon it.

Jacob accepts his dream as a divine confirmation to him of the birthright covenant made to his forefathers, the importance of which lies in the fact that he is to be the actual ancestor of the promised Christ Himself. He erects the stone as a cairn, Biblically called a pillar,[6] consecrating it with sacred vows, and anointing it with oil.

---

[6]   Meb Matstsebah means a monument or memorial. It is not the word used for the pillar or column of a building.

In a subsequent dream when in Mesopotamia, God on His side also confirms the stone as a witness, and bids him go back to it.[7] The stone thus became doubly sacred, as consecrated by God as well as Jacob. To Jacob it was a witness that the ancient promises made by God to his grandfather would be realized through him and his descendants.

Returning in after days to Bethel, Jacob erects a new and more permanent cairn, and by inference, confirmed by subsequent events, constitutes the original stone a family, and ultimately a national heirloom, which must always accompany him. Eventually he migrates to Egypt, and, on his deathbed, in conferring his patriarchal divinely-inspired prophetic blessings upon his sons, constitutes Joseph guardian of the stone.[8]

At the Exodus the stone in the care of Joseph's tribe of Ephraim, together with the bones of Joseph, is presumably carried with the Israelites. There is a suggestion that it may have been the "loose rock" struck by Moses for water. Once in Palestine Ephraim established a central seat of government at Shechem. Under David the stone is probably removed with the Ark to Jerusalem. In Solomon's Temple we find a coronation stand or seat described in our version

---

[7] Gen. xxxi. 11-14, and xxxv. I.

[8] This is at least a feasible interpretation of Gen. xiix. 22-25, an otherwise obscure passage, of which no commentary provides any satisfactory explanation.

as "a pillar," which, however, here means a raised stand or dais, not a column, for the king stood upon it, and which is claimed to be this stone. Kings of Judah are crowned upon it. The boy King, Joash, is taken from his secret hiding-place and proclaimed King standing upon it.[9] The usurper Athaliah is quick in consequence to recognize what is happening when she enters and cries "Treason." She sees him standing on the royal dais.

In carrying out his national reformation King Josiah solemnly reconsecrates himself and the nation to Jehovah standing on this dais—Jacob's stone.[10]

So much for the early part of the story.

From Jerusalem to Tara

The keystone, however, upon which the whole tradition with regard to the stone rests, lies in that part of the story that takes the stone from Jerusalem at the time of its destruction by Nebuchadnezzar to Tara in Ireland. Unless the departure from Jerusalem and ultimate arrival at Tara can be established, together with a reasonable explanation as to how the strange migration came about, the whole tradition falls to the ground.

---

[9] 2 Kings xi. 14. "On the accustomed dais," not as in the Authorised Version "*by* a pillar as the manner was."

[10] 2 Kings xxiii. 3, "on" not "by."

Its traditional arrival in Ireland rests upon the authority of ancient Irish records and traditions which teem with stories. A summary of which we give below.

The Biblical story of events at the time of the fall of Jerusalem when Jeremiah concealed the Ark, his forced departure to Tarpanhes in Egypt, and his migration thence to Spain and ultimately on to Ireland, have already been recorded in the main part of this work, and need no repetition.[11]

As already stated, ancient Irish history and traditions tell us of the coming to that land at about the time in question of an old man called Ollam Fodhla, accompanied by a royal princess, variously named Tamar Tephi or Tea Tephi, and an aged companion named Simon Brug. He brought with him a sacred stone, and a mysterious covered box.

The clans of Ireland were wont to elect a paramount chief bearing the title "Ardath," in much the same way as the ancient Britons elected a "Pendragon." The reigning Ardath at the time, head of one of the Danite clans, was Heremon[12] Eochaidh I, and his seat of government was Clothair, Co. Meath, subsequently called Tara, the glory of whose halls is sung by Moore in his Irish melodies.

---

[11] See p. 61 f.

[12] Heremon appears to have been a title borne by hereditary chieftains.

Ollam Fodhla on his arrival made his way to Clothair, presented the credentials he had brought with him, and was received with the highest honours. His influence resulted in a national reformation, and the establishment of a new code of laws. The marriage of Eochaidh to Tea Tephi was solemnly enacted over the stone by Ollam Fodhla.

Irish tradition asserts that Olam Fodhla was Jeremiah; that the princess was a daughter of Zedekiah the last king of Judah, and, therefore, Queen of the Jews in her own right; that Simon Brug was Jeremiah's scribe Baruch, who figures so much in Biblical history; that the stone was Jacob's pillow; and finally that the mysterious box was none other than the Ark of the Covenant, which latter tradition, however, has been shown to be erroneous.

Such in brief outline is the story that may be constructed connecting Jacob's pillow at Bethel with the Stone of Scone at Westminster.

It will be seen at a glance that the crux of the story is the identification of Ollam Fodhla with the Prophet Jeremiah.

The following points, some of which we have already recorded are certainly significant.

Ollam Fodhla has a Hebrew derivation and means Holy Prophet. Irish tradition asserts the identity, and Jeremiah or Jerry is perhaps the most popular of Irish names.

THE REMOVAL OF THE STONE OF SCONE
FROM EGYPT

(From the original painting by A. Forestier)

Reproduced by kind permission of the "Illustrated London News" from the Coronation Record number of King George V

That his influence caused a national reformation, and the establishment of a new code of law appears assured. The famous Four Courts of Dublin, burned down a few years ago, were decorated with large medallions of the world's greatest law-givers. They included Alfred, Solon, Confucius, Moses, and Ollam Fodhla.[13]

In his companion, Simon Brug, we may certainly recognize Baruch the scribe.

The names of Tamar or Tea Tephi are of Hebrew origin, Tamar being a popular Jewish name, while Tea means wanderer, and Tephi beauty.

It is significant that Clothair, the seat of government from this time was re-named Tara, the Hebrew *torah*, meaning "the law."

The burial-place of Jeremiah is claimed for two different places, the best authenticated being Old Castle not far from Tara, where a huge cairn of stones marks the spot, and a large carved stone is still pointed out as his judicial seat. Some thirty stones with strange markings upon them, lie here in the sepulchral chamber within the cairn. They have never yet been deciphered, but attempts to do so are now being made, and it is thought that the clue has been found.

---

[13]   It is fair to mention that more recent opinion docs not identify this Ollam Fodhla with Jercmiah. On the medallion he appears wcaring a crown, but Jeremiah was not crowned.

Whatever may be said of the story thus traced out, all will agree that it hangs together, and while evidence for some links may not be strong, others are clear.

Professor A. C. Ramsay examined the Coronation Stone in 1865, at the instance of Dean Stanley. It is dull reddish or purple calcareous sandstone, with slight chisel marks. He thought it somewhat resembled stone near Dunstaffnage, but as evidence is definite that it was brought thither from Ireland, this suggestion falls to the ground.

The assured modern part of the story of the stone enshrouds it with a sanctity that enhances the solemnity of a Coronation. How much more so if the one crowned upon it is in any way the inheritor of the Divine Covenant blessings enacted upon it.

The Coronation Stone has two large loose rings in eyes let into it at either end, by which it was carried. These are of some unrustable metal. The secret of treating metal so as permanently to prevent rusting seems to have been known to the ancients. The rings hang quite loosely from the eyes let into the stone. At first it would appear as if two poles were used, one of them passed through the ring at each end, so that four people would be required to carry the stone. These rings, however, when turned up, protrude above the top of the stone, enabling one pole to be passed through both rings across the top of the stone, enabling it to be carried by only two people. In preparation for King George V's coronation, the stone was temporarily removed from the Coronation Chair, and a photograph was taken of it. This discloses that a groove runs right across the stone from ring to ring. From its appearance this groove was not cut, but was clearly the result of friction of the pole passed across from ring to ring. Such an indentation and wearing away of the stone indicates the enormous amount of carrying that the stone was subjected to.

OLLAM FODHLA'S (JEREMIAH'S) CHAIR
Lough Crew Hill, near Oldcastle, co. Meath

THE CORONATION STONE

Photographed when removed from the Coronation
Chair in preparation for the Coronation of George VI

*Photograph reproduced by kind permission of the
Dean and Chapter of Westminster Abbey*

Now British, Scotch, and Irish records of the stone locate it at Tara, from whence 'it was transported in A.D. 498, by Fergus, first King of Argyle, to Dunstaffnage in Scotland, and thence to Iona in 565. From Iona it was removed to Scone near Perth, and finally by Edward I to Westminster.

Thus from Tara to Westminster covering some 1,500 years of history it was never carried to any appreciable extent. The mere removal from these places could not have caused the wearing away of the stone that is evident by friction of the pole used in constant carrying. This must have been the result of many months of continuous carrying prior to its arrival at Tara. The story of its journeying from Bethel in the time of Jacob, as traced out below, would account for its condition.

NOTE.—Proposals for and attempts at the excavation of the hill of Tara have from time to time been made. As we go to press, a report appears in the Press that a new attempt is about to be made by Harvard University, under the guidance of a leading British archaeologist. Tara is the property of the National Trust of Ireland, and is very jealously guarded as such. It is our earnest hope that the Irish will appreciate the importance of an excavation of the site, and will facilitate any movement to accomplish this.

OLLAM FODHLA'S (JEREMIAH'S) CAIRN
Lough Crew Hill, near Oldcastle, co. Meath

DESCRIPTION OF THE ARK AND ITS EARLY HISTORY

T HE Ark was constructed under Divine instructions, which are set out in detail in Exodus xxv. 10-22. It was an oblong chest 2 cubits in length by 1 in breadth and 1 in depth. The sacred cubit, distinguishable from the profane cubit, was 25 inches The Ark was, therefore, approximately 62 by 37 by 37 inches. It was made of acacia wood overlaid with gold. It was covered by a solid slab of gold, the thickness of which is not stated, called the Mercy-Seat. At either end were the solid Golden Cherubim, facing each other, and looking down upon the Mercy-Seat between them, and covering it with their outstretched wings. Two staves passing through golden rings were used for carrying it. When carried the Ark was covered with the veil which separated the Holy of Holies from the Holy Place, over which was a covering of badger skin, and this again was covered with a blue cloth.

The Ark was the receptacle of the two tables of stone containing the ten commandments, a pot of manna, to perpetuate the memory of the wilderness wandering, and Aaron's rod that budded (Heb. ix. 4).

The Ark as the symbol and witness of a Divine Presence in the midst of Israel played an important part in several historical events in the nation's history. At the time of the invasion of Palestine under Joshua, the Ark was carried in advance of the host to the edge of the water of the river Jordan, and when its waters were cut off, the Ark remained in the middle of the dry bed of the river until all had crossed.

At the capture of Jericho the Ark was carried in the midst of the procession round the city.

These two events established it in the eyes of the people as the Divine symbol of a Divine Presence. To the enemy and the outside world, it must have assumed the character of an idol, the form and appearance of which was unknown since it was never seen uncovered.

On the settlement of the land after the conquest we find the Tabernacle at Shiloh, and here the Ark seems to have remained during the period of the Judges.

In the time of Eli the Israelites suffered a reverse at the hands of the Philistines, and, recalling doubtless the part played by the Ark in the original invasion of the land under Joshua, the Ark was brought into the host to be misused as a kind of fetish to bring victory. Its presence brought dismay to the Philistine host, and only served to goad them to despairing valiance in the battle which followed. The Ark was captured and carried in triumph to their city Ashdod, the Philistines placed it in the temple of Dagon the fish-god. The idol was found lying shattered before it, and the city was smitten with a strange plague described as emerods. Gath and Ekron suffered similarly, and they decided to return the Ark to the Israelites. The Ark was placed on a new cart with suitable propitiatory offerings, and the oxen which drew it took the direct road for Beth-shemesh. The men of Beth-shemesh perpetrated a grave sacrilege by looking into the Ark, and we read of 50,070 men being smitten with instant death. This terrible judgment resulted in its removal to Kirjath-jearim, where it remained for twenty years.

David next had the Ark transported to Jerusalem, where he placed it in a special tent prepared for it. On the outbreak of Absalom's rebellion, David left Jerusalem. He was followed by Zadok the priest, with the Ark, but David bade him carry it back to the city. It found its final permanent resting-place in Solomon's Temple. In 1 Kings viii. 9 we read that at this time the Ark contained nothing but the two tables of stone. The pot of manna and Aaron's rod must, therefore, have been removed previous to this. From the reign of Solomon onwards we have no further mention of the Ark of the Covenant until the time of Josiah. In the course of his reformation he instructed the Levites to replace the Ark in its place in the Temple,[14] from which, we must conclude, it had been at some time previously removed, Josiah's predecessor had desecrated the Temple by the introduction of an idol, and it is probable, that owing to this profanity the priests had temporarily removed it to some chamber in the Temple.

The statement is of special importance as indicating that the Ark was still in its place in the Temple just prior to Nebuchadnezzar's capture of the city.

---

[14] 2 Chronicles xxxiii. 3.

THE SYMBOLISM
OF THE ARK

T HE title "Ark of the Covenant" implies that it was a visible witness to the Divine Covenant made by Jehovah with Israel. Enshrined in that Covenant was the promise of a coming Saviour of the world. The Ark, therefore, symbolized both by its construction and history the Person and work of the coming Christ.

Its Construction.—Made of acacia wood, overlaid with gold, it typified the human and Divine natures of Christ. The wood reflected the perishable human, and the gold the imperishable divine. It was never exposed to view, being covered with the veil, the badger skin, and the cloth of blue. The veil reflected Our Lord's incarnation, the badger skins His earthly humiliation and death, for the skins implied the death of the badger. Over all was the blue cloth, which alone would be outwardly visible, and represented the Divine Character which reflected His whole nature.

The fact that it was never exposed to view reminds us that the dual nature of Our Lord is mystery which is impenetrable, Attempts to penetrate it led to the Arian controversy followed by a host of further 'controversies down to the present day.

The Mercy-Seat stained by the blood of the sacrifice of atonement typified the work of reconciliation between God and man accomplished by Christ.

The Ark contained the stone tables of the law, and symbolized that the law broken by man, is lost in Christ who provides a new Covenant or Testament.

The two Cherubim looking down upon the Mercy-Seat stained with the blood of the sacrifice of atonement, typified God's eye always upon the sacrifice wrought by Christ's death, by which man gains mercy.

The mysterious "Shekinah Light," which rested on the Mercy-Seat between the Cherubim, was a visible evidence of a Divine Presence.

No one except the High Priest ever penetrated into the Holy of Holies, the dwelling place of the Ark, and he entered but once a year to offer the blood of Atonement. Christ alone can intercede with God for man, and offers His blood in reconciliation.

Its History.—While the construction of the Ark reflects the Person and mission of Christ, its history reflects His work among men.

The place of the Ark was in the midst of the camp. Christ is ever in our midst. On one occasion, however, the Ark went before them in a three days' journey "to search out a resting-place for them." This may be a reflection of the three days' journey of death and resurrection, by which Christ found a resting-place for man.

We next have the Ark in the bed of the River Jordan. So long as it remained there the waters remained cut off, and there it remained until "all the people were clean passed over." Christ is the author and finisher of faith. His presence will constrain the forces of evil until all who trust in Him have passed safely.

The story of the capture of Jericho is rich in its lessons. Jericho means "fragrant with spices," and represents the allurements of the world. The Ark was carried round day by day in the centre of the long procession of warriors. With its skyblue covering it would be most conspicuous to the people of Jericho. The lesson of the story is that we are not to fight against the world, but to carry Christ with us, and His presence visible in our lives will keep temptation from attacking us, and ultimately cause its defeat.

In a similar way in every incident in which the Ark played a part there may be traced some illustration of the ways and work of Christ.

THE ROYAL HOUSE
OF BRITAIN

O UR study of the mystery of the Fate of the Ark of the Covenant has led us into the region of Irish traditions associated with Tara in Co. Meath, the ancient seat of the early kings or Ardaths of Ireland, where perhaps the clue to the secret hiding-place in Mount Nebo is to be found.

The value of these traditions rests entirely upon the identity of Ollam Fodhla with Jeremiah the Prophet. If this be accepted, then it follows that Tamar Tephi must also be accepted to have been a daughter of Zedekiah, and the "stone wonderful" which he brought with him, now the Stone of Scone at Westminster, to have been Jacob's pillow at Bethel.

The acceptance of these three identities leads on to a startling conclusion, namely, that the marriage of Tamar Tephi to Eochaidh I implies the transference of the royal line of David and the Kings of Judah to the British Isles, where it may be traced without serious challenge down to King George VI. Tamar Tephi, if she was indeed Zedekiah's daughter, was heiress in her own right to the throne of her ancestors.

On May 11, 1937, the day before the Coronation of King George VI, *The Times* issued an admirable Coronation Supplement. This included a whole page pedigree tracing the Royal line back to Egbert (A.D. 802-839) in English history, and Kenneth MacAlpin (A.D.. 832-860) in Scottish history. It also informs us that MacAlpin was descended from Fergus Mor MacErc (A.D. 498501), who was first King of Argyle. Between Fergus and MacAlpin, who was first King of United Scotland, Scottish history gives us fourteen kings of Argyle, whose names, however, are not included in *The Times* list.

If Tamar Tephi was indeed a daughter of Zedekiah, and married Eochaidh I, then the Royal line of Britain may be traced in continuous descent from Jacob, with whom we naturally begin since he consecrated the stone at Bethel.

St. Matthew i. and St. Luke iii. give us the pedigree of Christ. The names from Jacob to Jesse the father of David may be regarded as the Heads of the Tribe of Judah, to which tribe Jacob conferred the sovereignty over Israel, in his prophetic dying blessings on his twelve sons. "The sceptre shall not depart from Judah," he said, "nor a lawgiver from between his feet, until

Shiloh come" (Gen. xliv. 10). This prophecy was realized when David became King over all Israel on the death of Saul.

After the death of Solomon, David's son, a severance in the nation took place. It became split into the two Kingdoms of Israel, comprising ten tribes, and Judah including the tribe of Benjamin.

The succession of nineteen kings of Judah down to Zedekiah is recorded in the books of Kings and Chronicles.

Zedekiah disappears, a blind captive, at Babylon, his sons having been slain before his eyes, before they were put out, obviously to destroy all hope of a Royal male succession. His daughters, however, the Bible tells us were rescued by Jeremiah, one of whom, as we have seen, was Tamar Tephi, or Tea Tephi. Ancient Irish records, to which reference has been made, give us the names of fifty-four Ardaths, or head-kings of Ireland, springing from her marriage with Eochaidh I, Ardath of Ireland. The last of these, Eogan, left no son, but a daughter named Earca, who married a sub-king of North-East Ireland, named Muireadhach, and the Crown of Ireland passed to a collateral branch.

Fergus, the first King of Argyle, mentioned in *The Times list* was a son of Earca—and Muireadhach. He led an expedition of conquest from Northern Ireland to Argyle, and within two years had established the

Kingdom of Scotland, better known as Argyle. The Scots who ultimately gave their name to the country were the people whom Fergus led from Northern Ireland, now known as Ulster. After establishing the Kingdom of Argyle, Fergus sent across to Tara for the Coronation Stone on which his mother's fifty-four ancestors had been crowned. The Royal line had passed to him through his mother, Earca. He had, therefore, the right to claim the stone, and transfer it to the seat of the new Kingdom of the ancient sovereign line.

Under Alpin, the 14th in succession of the Kings of Argyle, war broke out between Argyle, or the Scots, and the Picts of the Southern half of Scotland, and his son, Kenneth MacAlpin, became the first King of United Scotland. *The Times* gives the complete list of thirty-eight kings of Scotland from Kenneth MacAlpin to Mary Queen of Scots. Her son, James VI of Scotland, became James I of England. The following is the summary of the Royal succession from Jacob to King George VI, as passing through the Scottish and Irish lines of Kings. The Royal pedigree may also be traced through the Tudors.

Jacob and Chieftains of the paramount tribe of Judah to Jesse	11
Kings of United Israel—David and Solomon	2
Kings of Judah to Zedekiah	19
Kings or Ardaths of Ireland	54
Kings of Argyle	14
Kings of United Scotland	38
Kings of the United British Isles	15
	153

Students of Biblical prophetic numbers will at once appreciate the significance of this figure. We subjoin the full list of names:

The Royal Succession

JACOB

Chieftains of the Sovereign tribe of Judah—10.
Judah, Phares, Hezron, Aram, Aminadab, Naashon, Salmon, Boaz, Obed, Jesse.

Kings of United Israel—2.
David, Solomon.

Kings of Judah—19.
Rehoboam, Abijah, Asa, Jehoshaphat, Jehoram, Ahaziah, Joash, Amaziah, Uzziah, Jotham, Ahaz, Hezekiah, Manasseh, Amon, Josiah, Jehoahaz, Jehoiakim, Jehoiachin, Zedekiah.

Ardaths or Head-Kings of Ireland—54.
Tamar Tephi or Tea Tephi, daughter of Zedekiah, married Eochaidh I, Ardath of Ireland, from whence we have the following succession as given from ancient records by Glover, Pineda, Massey, Milner, Grimaldi, etc.

Tephi, married Heremon Eochaidh I, Irial Faidh, Eijthriall, Follain, Tighernmas, Eanbotha, Smiorguil, Fiachadh Labhruine, Aongus Oilbhuagach, Maoin, Rotheachta, Dein, Siorna Saoghalach, Oiliolla Olchaoin, Giallchadh, Nuadha Fionn Fail, Simon Breac, Muriadhach Bolgrach, Fiachadh Tolgrach, Duach Laighrach, Eochaidh Buillaig, Ugaine More the Great, Cobhthach Caolbreag, Meilage, Jaran Gleofathach, Conla Cruaich, Cealgach, Oiliolla Caisfhiaclach, Eochaid Foltleathan, Aongus Tuirimheach, Eanda Aighnach, Labhra Luire, Blathachta, Eamhna, Easamhuin Eamhna, Roighneim Ruadh, Finlogha, Finn, Eochaidh Feidhlioch, Bias Fineamhnas, Lughaidh Riebdearg, Criomhthan Niadhnar, Fioraidhach Fionfachtnach, Fiachadh Fionchudh, Tuathal Teachtman. Feidhlimhioh Reachtmar, Conn Ceadchadhach, Art Aonfhir, Cormac Ulfhada, m. Cithne Ollamhdha, Cairbre Liffeachaire, Fiachadh Streabhthuine, Muirreadhach Tireach, m. Muirion, Eochaidh Moihmeodhain, Niall of the Nine Hostages, Eogan, Muireadhach, m. Earca.

Kings of Argyle—14.

Fergus More, Dongard, Conran, Constantine I, Aidan, Eugene, Donald, Dongard or Donregarth, Eugene IV, Findan, Eugene V, Ethafind, Achaias, Alpin,

Sovereigns of Scotland—98.

Kenneth MacAlpin, Constantine II, Aedh, Eocha, Donald I, Constantine III, Malcolm I, Indulf, Duff, Colin, Kenneth II, Constantine IV, Kenneth III, Malcolm II, Duncan I, MacBeth, Lulach, Malcolm III, Donald II (Duncan II), Edgar, Alexander I, David I, Malcolm IV, William the Lion, Alexander II, Alexander III, Margaret, John Balliol, Robert I Bruce, David II (Edward Balliol), Robert II, Robert III, James I, James II, James III, James IV, James V, Mary Queen of Scots.

Sovereigns of Great Britain—15.

James VI of Scotland and I of England, Charles I, Charles IT, James II, William and Mary, Anne, George I, George II, George III, George IV, William IV, Victoria, Edward VII, George V, George VI.

We omit the name of Edward VIII since he refused consecration and coronation on the stone at Westminster.